The Bible Is a Goldmine

God and Clarice Smith

TEACH Services, Inc.
PUBLISHING
www.TEACHServices.com • (800) 367-1844

World rights reserved. This book or any portion thereof may not be copied or reproduced in any form or manner whatever, except as provided by law, without the written permission of the publisher, except by a reviewer who may quote brief passages in a review.

The author assumes full responsibility for the accuracy of all facts and quotations as cited in this book. The opinions expressed in this book are the author's personal views and interpretations, and do not necessarily reflect those of the publisher.

This book is provided with the understanding that the publisher is not engaged in giving spiritual, legal, medical, or other professional advice. If authoritative advice is needed, the reader should seek the counsel of a competent professional.

Copyright © 2023 Clarice Smith
Copyright © 2023 TEACH Services, Inc.
ISBN-13: 978-1-4796-1514-8 (Paperback)
ISBN-13: 978-1-4796-1515-5 (ePub)
Library of Congress Control Number: 2023905972

Scripture taken from the King James Version (KJV). Public domain.

Table of Contents

Acknowledgements	viii
The Bible Is a Goldmine	9
Road Is Narrow	10
What Do I Find in the Bible Goldmine?	12
Do You Know What the Bible Is About?	13
Didn't Know We Were Far from Him	14
A Friend	15
Isn't This True	16
Life Is a Journey	17
Drink Scriptures as Milk	19
Years Come, Years Go	20
In the Goldmine	21
As I Study	22
There's a Lot	23
A Very Different New Person	24
No Other Book	25
Bible Hard to Read	27
Pearl of Sweetness	28
T-H-E W-O-R-D O-F G-O-D I	29
The Bible Open Wide	30

Bible Takes Me Places	31
Untitled I	33
Every Scripture Has a Lesson	34
Goldmine Just Ahead	35
ABCs Sentence	37
In the Goldmine	38
T-H-E W-O-R-D O-F G-O-D II	39
Promises	40
Harmony	42
Only Book!	43
Praise	45
Bible Inspired and Inspires	47
Cross of Calvary	48
In His Word	49
Precious Gift	50
He Is God	51
B-I-B-L-E	52
Idols	56
Beauty	57
Abundant Life	58
There Is No Other	59
The Messiah	60
Sabbath Worship Home	61
COVID-19	62
Lord, What Can I Do?	63

Praise for *The Bible is a Goldmine*

"I absolutely loved this book! It was truly beautiful and brings you closer to God. My favorite poem is "There's a Lot"—that one has so much meaning and goes along with the title of this book: **The Bible is a Goldmine**.

"I also very much liked that it included the bible verses to go along with the Poems. This book is truly tremendous, and I would rate this book a 10 out of 10! Highly recommend this book to all God's Believers! Hallelujah! Amen!"

~ Tonya Thompson, homemaker

"**The Bible is a Goldmine** is an inspiring collection of poems written by Clarice Smith. She is a lover of God, and it shows in her poems. Each page will point you to our loving Heavenly Father. I loved the first poem and didn't want to put it down. May God so bless you as you enjoy this wonderful book."

~ Eda Stoll, Cook, homemaker, Wife, Mother, and Nana

"I loved the poem "Filled to the Brim." It is so true of this book, an inspirational read about God's love and grace that he has for each one of us. Love the corresponding bible references, each one fits the poem. You can use this book for a bible study. God bless the writer and the reader."

~ Vonna Myers, machine operator

"Clarice Smith has written a poetry book to remind us that the Bible is the very word of God! Filled with heart-felt thoughts from over a lifetime of following Jesus this book will challenge you to "dig deep" into the treasure trove of His word for yourself. Don't be fooled by the "simple" language, the message is far from simple! As you read your heart will be touched—and anyone else you share it with—of the great love God has for you...waiting in His word!"

~ Cheri Typaldos

The Bible Now	64
Today Now	65
Now That You Are Saved	66
Devotions Outline, Galatians 3:1–25	69
Change My Mind	72
Filled to the Brim	74
Thanksgiving	77
Love Story is Love Letter	78
Into Goldmine Go!	80
Psalm 51 for Today	82
91st Psalm Shadow	83
My Friend, Don	84
Message to Tell	86
Message, Part 2	88
Haven't Thought	89
G-R-A-C-E	90
Bible Written	91
As We Study a Bit	93
Postscript	94

Acknowledgements

Not one poem would be written if God had not given me the talent. In 1954, my goals for four years: to leave a poem, short note, or story. No, not even a joke.

Behold, in 1963, during adult church teaching, a poem, "Home," found elsewhere in the book, was given to me.

God's promises are true. I claimed Psalm 37:4: "Delight thyself also in the Lord: and he shall give thee the desires of thine heart."

May I take a few minutes of your time? Don, Pat, Viv, Doris, and the Hatch family encouraged me to put my poems into a book. "Not God's timing. If it is to be, He will make it known to me." If one person who has wandered away finds God and believes, this book's timing will be confirmed.

All praise, glory, and thank You goes to God's Son. Hallelujah, Amen.

The Bible Is a Goldmine

Worth more than diamonds,
Shines brighter than the sun,
Newer than morning news,
More fruit than a fruit cake.
Speaks loud ever so soft and clear;
Love contains blessings overflowing;
Verses so old but ever so new,
One message all the way through.
Telling us all about Thee. We need to repent!
God's Son did it all for us.
We cannot save ourselves;
God's Son loves you and I.
We eat not the Bible,
But the Bible eats us.
Always speaking, talking, and telling
Jesus loves us enough.
To go back to His heavenly throne.
He left us a map to show the way,
"The truth, the life, and the way" —John 14:6.
Left examples: to pray; He is the light.
Stop signs: a path wrong or right.
One path leads to His love, mercy, and grace.
Looking o'er this poem? Ask me,
Which path leads to a Goldmine?
Which path am I on?

Road Is Narrow

The road is narrow not wide;
When the Holy Spirit comes in to abide,
Satan throws fiery darts our way.
Ephesians 6:16

God turns them around to refine the way.

Our life showeth forth His light.
His salt: Our wrong He makes right.
Satan tempts: God uses as testing.

How am I doing and listening?
Many times I find myself unaware;
God gave me His Armor to wear.
Ephesians 6:11

The greatest need I need is faith and love;
Cometh not from me but just a gift from above.

[written in 1965]

What Do I Find in the Bible Goldmine?

ABCs, Yeah?
Atonement
Blood
Cross
Deliverance
Eternal
Faith
God
Heaven
Inspire
Jesus
Knowledge
Love
Messiah
No, Not One
Obedience
Prayer
Queen
Righteousness
Sinner (me)
Trust
Under His Wings
V-I-C-T-O-R-Y
"Whiter than Snow"
X stands in Greek for Jesus
Y you and I
Z Zeal or Zealous
"Did it!"

[written in 1992]

Do You Know What the Bible Is About?

Neither do I, but know it's filled
With faith, not doubt.
Tells us things rather good or bad,
Tells us about God, and His all
He had He gave.

Tells us sacrifices and offerings in O.T. weren't enough.
Ask to give then praises, singing, thanksgiving as such.
So many verses and stories to follow,
Others, if heeded, our life would be hollow.

Throughout weaved there in there is Holy Spirit;
In the N.T. faith and works fit;
God's power seems to flow through us.
James 2:20–24
To overcome and when we lift Christ up
We are amazed, and don't like to be called a sinner, you and I.

[written in 1977]

Didn't Know We Were Far from Him

We cannot deny
Most all the books within
Written years apart,
Yet, they harmonize; same love and unity of God impart.

Yes, verses to celebrate on
Special occasions.
Even brings connection so,
We accept His salvation
When hurting, lonely, sad,
Fearing and sickness;
Power cometh forth turning
Sadness to gladness.

I know I haven't even hit the surface,
Words written to worship in His service;
Words hid in heart when young, pop out when old.
Yes, the best Book as fresh as the newspaper we hold.

I'm sure you can add more—
Revelation 3:20 find Jesus at the door.
He is Divine and the true vine—John 15;
In due time works things fine—Romans 8:28.

A Friend

A Friend, a Friend
Has no beginning, no end.
Knows me better than I,
The good, the bad;
As I confess, He lifts me up when sad.

Knows my hidden secrets and long life's way,
Like Adam and Eve wanted to hide today.
But He said, "I forgive you;" spoke loving, "I love you."
Yes! He saved me by His GRACE! He lifted me, too.

My Friend LOVES everyone,
He is GOD's only Son—John 3:16;
This is what my Friend did—Romans 5:8,
So, we could be—2 Corinthians 5:17.

He speaks today to us—Matthew 11:28;
Always with us—Matthew 28:20.
Continue on in Scripture—Hebrews 13:5;
More proof (today)—2 Corinthians 6:2.

[written in 1977]

Isn't This True?

Life is a mess here;
It is same everywhere.
Like me can you say, "I didn't know Jesus Christ loved me so much"?

I was a sinner in need of His touch.
Maybe you never heard before,
Or didn't know He is the Door.
If I just told, you may not believe,
I'll show you Scripture you may want to receive.

God says His Words:
2 Timothy 3:16
Psalm 119:105
Psalm 12:6

If you believe, doesn't it make sense?
Romans 5:8
John 3:16

[written in 1968]

Life Is a Journey

Kind of rocky, weak, and self-seeking,
Satan leads his clever disobeying.
Wanted to be like GOD with power;
We, too, do our thing, control and devour.

God tells us we all are sinners far from Him;
We believers—when unbelievers did the same—sin.
God sent forth His Son;
Sinners could be cleansed one by one.

His Son's blood is our living sacrifice;
Wages of sin is death, Jesus paid our price—
Romans 3:10 and Romans 3:23.
Christ Jesus paid "What dearly price?"—Romans 6:23;

We cannot do a thing.
No amount of money we can bring
If we worked around the clock 24/7,
Never could do or get us to heaven.
How then? Believe; repent to His Son.
God had the answer—John 3:16.

[written in 1972]

Drink Scriptures as Milk

Holy Spirit will teach and guide;
Allow Him to work—flesh must step aside.
Let His Holy Spirit in to complete God's mission—

Which will never get done
Till everyone in the world
Comes to God's Son,
Or Jesus returns to Earth.

The dead in Christ arise first;
We alive, hungry, and thirsty, second.
Now, if you know not Christ, it is not to late;
Till Christ comes, we are under His Grace.

Known as grace time or period:
Invitation—"Come"—Matthew 11:28;
Still time—2 Corinthians 6:2;
Door open—Revelation 3:20.

Years Come, Years Go

But I think now God Almighty is the true God;
His begotten Son is Savior and Lord.

He cleaned me up that day
I confessed and did pray.
The load carried was gone;
Years come and years go, believers know.

Jesus, God's Son, washes white as snow.
Isaiah 1:18

A new person made whole.
2 Corinthians 5:17
New outlook from sin,
New thoughts, new ways, new actions because of Him
Who knew no sin,
And in our heart lives within.

Nothing ever changes, always the same!
The Bible, God, Jesus, Holy Spirit.
Years come, years go.

[written in 1976]

In the Goldmine

As I try to line up God and my poems,
More poems come; two lines and I know a poem's on its way.
Stop, find pencil or pen, need to write right away.
If not, I lost it, can't remember even as I pray.

Sometimes they become so deep,
In a notebook I want to keep.
The two-edged sword speaks—
Full of love and faith, not doubt.
Hebrews 4:12

I found more by His touch,
And blessings unfold as He fills my cup.
He giveth me faith to walk on;
His Holy Spirit brings forth a song.

[written in 1992]

As I Study

As I study and read,
Hunger continues as I feed.
In the verses grow a little bit more;
He closes and opens to me another door.

Sometimes, somehow I find deep things
As His Holy Spirit does bring.
An axe splits things in two,
Reminds surrendering me as well as you.
God showeth what He doesn't like,
Confessing a wrong, He makes right.

A hammer used many a way;
Scriptures memorized in a heart stay.
Find ourselves in a hard spot?
That verse or verses helped a lot.

Soon may silently hear
He that has an ear
A Word of God does say, "GO."
Matthew 28:18–20

There's a Lot

In a Goldmine there's a lot of digging,
In the Bible there's a lot of finding.
Both do the same searching;
The Bible is a Goldmine
But rest assured, answers in the Bible hold.

Oh, some may take a long time,
But digging and searching questions find
Bible searchers leave with a smile,
While gold diggers move down the line.

Bible diggers find a spade or two;
Flesh yielded to the Holy Spirit true.
Flesh entwines soon as dedication,
Surrendering after finding His salvation.

Bible diggers find a block or something;
That something draws nearer to God.
Find Him Savior and Lord.
Each person not the same as entered Goldmine.

[written June 26, 2020]

A Very Different New Person

Unknown but same;
Something changed in Jesus' name.
Later, often hear in a sweet, sweet voice,
"I want you to go, but you need to make the choice,"
saith the Lord.

My, oh my, a sinner, a whole bag of rags.
Isaiah 64:6
Who is, was made white as snow;
Found "Christ's righteousness,"
The Bible says.

For words
Unbelievable
Made believable.

Thanks again, Holy Spirit, "Amen!"

No Other Book

No other book speaks to us;
No other changes by a touch.
Old Testament and New
Tell one story.

Written centuries, many years apart,
Same word and same message impart.
"Repent!" Turn back to God."
Even right today we have the Savior as the Lord.

All the prophets would say it; the Messiah did
Constantly obey God's will.
He was open and not hid.
Promises were kept and many healed;
Today we don't do as we feel.

Our flesh never does enter in;
We are humans and fall into sin.
His Holy Spirit teaching us to walk His way
As We read, study, do each day.

No other book makes us kneel
Nor say, "Believe" and Jesus sealed.
Nor does it say, "To accept and believe;"
If we confess, the armor of God receive.

Oh, His gifts He wants us to have;
His Son willingly God gave.
Have you ever read with so much love?
God spoke to His Son as landed a dove.
Matthew 3:16–17

I could go on and so could you,
All we learn and can experience too.
Yes, gone sunk in lake of forgetfulness
As He forgave life's mess.

Do you believe the Bible is like no other book
That plants feet upon a solid foundation?
Our heart can be cleansed by the Great Divine;
We are His branches clinging to the Vine.

Bible Hard to Read

The Bible is so hard to read.
Names can't pronounce,
Can't follow every war,
Tells as is and as was.

V-I-C-T-O-R-Y in battle if stayed
True to God.
Tells our God loved and cared for them.
From the very first beginning, He hated sin,
In a Book hard to read.

Has redeemed and planted numerous seed;
As read on and on,
They for the Messiah yearn and long;
Always wander away and almost hear David's Song.

We, too, must confess we are or were far from God.
Bible does say we sinners need "Savior, the Lord."
Read Romans Chapter 3 although hard to read and understand;
Isaiah 53, whole chapter planted delivering seed. "Amen!"

[written in 1963]

Pearl of Sweetness

The Root of Jesse
The Bud of Aaron
The Vine of God
We are branches of Jesus,
Faith of Abraham from Seed is us.
Seed of David,
Prophets cry, "Repent!"

As a flower blooms in every nation,
Pearl of sweetness is salvation;
Radiance as angels sing, "Rejoice!"

[written in 1965]

THE WORD OF GOD I

The Word of God
Has lived on and on;
Every page is inspired.

World men tried to destroy;
Old Testament tells as was
Right down to our time,
Days, men try to water it down.

Often find Satan in sheep clothing;
Faith, grace, and love does abound.

God, men say, is "dead."
Our world is waxing worse;
Day by day, believers need to stand.

Notice men will not destroy,
Satan will be history—
Gone.

God is God, He will have last word;
God is in control.

Why not join Jesus' flow—His flock?

[written 1973]

The Bible Open Wide

The Bible open wide,
Son of God is the Vine
I found in my Goldmine,
And His Holy Spirit wants to abide.

As at home I study more,
Holy Spirit helps me to store.
I want to learn all I can,
Absorb in my heart like a sponge,
Drink Scriptures through a straw.

Pen what I want to keep,
Memory verse or verses I want to file away,
Eating Scripture, I might grow.

And be ready when I hear, "Go;"
Onward the message, so many will believe,
And sinners far from God may receive.
This is what I see when Bible is open wide.

[written in 1967]

Bible Takes Me Places

The Bible takes me to places,
Every experience by His grace;
Somewhere in Scriptures I relate;
Message: "It is never too late."

Maybe His sermon while I am in church,
Longed for answer as I hunger and thirst.
I might come, feeling not so good, kind of blue
As I sit in the pew.

Or someone's testimony lifted me up,
Tells experience of God's touch.
Like Paul and disciples traveled a lot,

From a map, find the plot.
Experiences right there to review,
Jesus spoke and gave parables for them, me and you,
As I search in the Goldmine, lots to chew.

[written in 1983]

Untitled I

I may sit in a chair or lie in bed,
Not sleeping but traveling instead.
Walking with Peter, Paul or whomsoever may be
by the Sea of Galilee,
Or see Zacchaeus climbing up the tree.
Whatever Scripture I seem to read,
Traveling with whomsoever planting God's seed.

Every Scripture Has a Lesson

In the Bible as I read, I see
There's a lesson for little ol' me,
Waking me up to God's truth,
If claimed may bring in Jesus' fruit.

Perchance, you have set on His salvation;
Maybe you need a rededication.
A Scripture calling out to me to share today,
Or draw someone unsaved, I pray.

His Holy Spirit wants to work to impart
As He gently touches my heart.
"Clarice, I saw the sin!"
Oh, I must confess that to Him.

We may even find His deeds and acts become part of us.

[written in 1974]

Goldmine Just Ahead

As I travel along,
I am so weak;
God is so strong,
Goldmine just ahead.

Can I make it? "No! Must stop instead."
But I know what I must do.

Close my eyes, rest a moment or two;
Call upon God—that's what I must do.

I hear a hammer pound;
I know grace does abound—Romans 5:20.
With a whisper I must get in shape,
My God is real, not a fake.

My life going fast as a whirl wheel,
Spiritual matter comes by each day, not how you feel.
Feeling reaction gets us nowhere;
It's not flesh but power cometh from somewhere.
Scissors cut and snap away,
Jesus teaches us to pray.
Must stop, need piece of candy so sweet,
Need to stop again, kneel at Jesus' feet.

Hear a bell in the distance a-ringing?
Ask, am I witnessing, another person bringing?
As I travel along in the Goldmine,
No gold, but all things are found—Roman 8:28.

As a-digging away each day,
Am I hearing angels singing away?
A sinner has come,
A sinner entered God's kingdom;
Now that is "Victory Day."
In the Goldmine stop to pray.
[written in 1999]

ABCs Sentence

Assurance or insurance do I need?
Bible—if heed—may plant a seed.
Christ is the answer for you and I;
Devotions help us see the need, Christ crucified.
Every Scripture can speak;
Faith we need, not doubt keep.
God and truly Lord,
"Heaven or Hell," says the Lord.
Invitation given 24/7—Matthew 11:28.
Jesus, God's Son, leads us to Heaven;
Key: "Yes!" opens all spiritual matter.
Love is our Bible, a love letter.
Message: "Repent," greatest of all;
"None be left out," is Jesus' call;
Omnipotent God sees all.
Pray from the heart when on Jesus we call;
Quietness calms and rests our soul.
Righteousness is in Christ, makes us whole;
Salvation, first step for all who are believers,
Trust and obey, second step to all receivers.

Under His wings we belong.
"Victory in Christ" is more than a song;
Whiter than snow to all who believe.
X in Greek is Christ, whom we receive;
You and I must stand firm on the solid foundation,
Zeal and zealous after salvation.
[written in 1975]

In the Goldmine

"T-H-E H-O-L-Y S-P-I-R-I-T"
In the Goldmine,
Acrostic I did find.
(Take title letters, run down.)

Trinity Creator before
Heaven and Earth,
Eternity with no end.

Holy Spirit sent by God,
Omnipotent and only—Revelation 19:6.
Love is who God is;
"Yeah!" This is only the beginning.

Sent to teach, correct, and guide;
Path to follow as the Son leads.
Inspires all believers and servants;
Rest assured we need the Holy Spirit.
In the stable born of virgin birth,
The Son of God, the Messiah, came to Earth.

[written in 1973]

THE WORD OF GOD II

The Word of God—
He speaks even today;
Every word is, was inspired.
Worldly men tried to destroy—Jeremiah 36:32.
Old Testament tells as was,
Right down to our time.
Love and unity constantly abound;
Day by day, false teachers water Word of God down.

Often, in sheep's clothing, Satan leads—Matthew 7:15.
Faith, love, and grace abound—Romans 5:20.

"God is dead," worldly folks are saying.
Our world is waxing worse;
Day by day, believers should stand firm.

Our feet are grounded on a solid foundation—2 Timothy 2:19,
1 Corinthians 3:11.

I was asked on Sabbath, January 20, 2010, to have a poem on "Promises" by the 10:45 service. My reply, "I can't, but I will pray."

Promises

So true is the song we just sung,
Promises—God filled His Word full of them.
Written in Old Testament right up to now,
Even now, today, He gives promises true.

He promised the Messiah one day would come;
He came to us so we may be one in His kingdom.
He gave to all many promises,
No matter what we face.

Promises come by His faith and grace,
The promise just when we need,
Psalms, Hebrews, Job, Jeremiah, and many more to heed.
Yes, Passover and Easter past and gone;
V-I-C-T-O-R-Y came to us early morn.
The promise, "I will rise the third day,"
Jesus said o'er and o'er as walked the way;
No one believed; no one understood.

Till Jesus arose and was seen in neighborhood;
We don't have to see Him,
We know He took our sin;
Yes, His promises are true.

Harmony

Harmony is found in the Bible all the way through;
Found in Genesis to Revelation it is so true.
When God placed man upon the Earth,
He created Adam in His image first,
Then, later, a woman, for a helpmate.
Soon sin of disobedience came: We can relate.
From Genesis to Revelation,
God pours out His wonderful love.
Find in Scriptures sacrifice requires blood from heaven above;
God sent His only begotten Son upon the scene.
All are wrapped up in Him it seems.
Old Testament as Moses taught,
We only, His people, were the beginning.
His only Son fulfilled the Ten Commandments: the Law,
With no sin, no error, not even a slight flaw.

Old Testament prophets told what Messiah would do and be,
God's Son fulfilled prophecy.
Yet that's not the end,
Today we benefit from HIM, Amen! Amen!
Yes, He is returning, says, o'er and o'er again,
God and His Son's love never ends.
Read from Genesis to Revelation,
His only Son made a way for our salvation.

Do you see harmony?
Not too late for you.
Matthew 11:28 says, "Come in."
Also, "Salvation today,"
In 2 Corinthians 6:2.
Tells how in the last book—Revelation 3:20.

[written in 1969]

Only Book!

The only Book draws dearer and nearer,
Daily in devotion find nearer and dearer.
Written way back when was, even today is,
Not coated over but is alive.
See each person: the good, the bad.
Yes, the "Best Book" one can have—
The Holy Bible, the Holy Writ—
Old and New Testaments fit.

Too bad in some homes sit
Collecting dust, sitting on shelf.
Why not bring it forth and read for yourself?
Each and every chapter tell something about God,
Love poured out by Savior as Lord.

Even speaks about end time in O.T. and N.T.;
We need not fear any of it.
God will help us, believers,
His Holy Spirit help it all fit.
I, that's me, probably be first to say,
"Oh, no," like Peter, the rooster crowed away.

But I'm truly sure I can lean on His foundation,
Little by little, may I have grown in His salvation.
One thing I know, I can't lean on flesh;
Time will tell when facing end time mess.

Matthew 24, 1 Timothy 4 are just the beginning;
These scriptures and others seeing.
Who would believe what happened in America,
January 6, 2021?
And days following, now March 5, 2021,
With chiefs of police arrested, one by one.

Look at news or pick up a newspaper,
Everywhere is getting worse.
Noah's time like rehearse
For a play, but true life is worse and worse.

COVID-19 takes lives every day;
May Christians pray and pray;
Be close to God each day.
Witness, bringing others to God's way.
Help where help be needed;
Fulfill John 15, if we would rely on Christ the Vine,
And we branches are seeded; John 15 "Read!"

[written in 1972]

Praise

Praise is another word for hello.
Don't we greet one another with that?
So, why not say, "Hello" to Our Savior the Lord?
Nor forget to say, "Thank You, God."

The plan, His beautiful creation,
He gave His only Son for our salvation.
Victories to overcome Satan's ways,
Beautiful verses along life's way.

Gave us His life so we can walk anew;
His Holy Spirit, most useful tool.
Sent and sending blessings to enjoy,
Enter in singing, "Rejoice! Rejoice!"

God inherits praise.
If we don't, creation will.

The rocks go swish splash,
The birds early or late tweet-tweet.
Trees sway and whistle,
Animals praise in their different voices.

Trees cut just right make cheerful notes;
Waters splash; they praise God in their way day by day.
How about us? Same, or only worship day when we come and say?
Praise from me as well as you today.

Bible Inspired and Inspires

The Bible inspired by His voice and hand—2 Timothy 3:16
Today works in each believer His way and
Leads and guides overseas or right here,
Spreading His special love everywhere.

Like Paul and disciples met every need—
Read John 15—He wants every believer to plant His seed.
If He calls and we wait too long,
May give to another a sad song.

No two people are alike or doing same,
But get it done in Jesus' name.
He fills our soul with joy unspeakable,
As we seek, ask, and pray, find delightful!

Bible always encourages, inspires, and lifts up;
We know not when Jesus will touch.

[written in 1972]

Cross of Calvary

The cross of Calvary—what the Bible is all about,
Christ coming to believers in faith, not doubt,
Proclaiming God's awesome love for all to see,
Paying "wages of sin," restoring fellowship for us to Thee.

God arose Him from the grave, one day,
Promise fulfilled; He is Truth, Life, and the Way.
That's the meaning of the cross of Calvary,
Bond with Satan is broken, and we are free.
"Hallelujah! Amen!"

[written July 14, 1963]

In His Word

In His Word I find I am nothing;
My flesh of rags to Him not anything.
Belong to Satan full of sin;
"Hopeless? No!" Believe, repent;
Accept there's hope within.

In His Word I can be something,
Only as I confess to Christ and cling.
Nothing in the world is worth keeping;
To grow in Him, must keep seeking.

In His Word He can make one whole,
Bring faith and love to a soul.
Teaching me to pray first,
Open my Bible, He quenches thirst.

In His Word I find Him light;
His Spirit takes wrong and makes it right.
Years ago, I walked in darkness,
But as a believer, I found gladness.

In Him there's joy and contentment;
"Love" is His commandment.
Faith is needed day by day,
Trusting Christ, He is the way—John 14:6.

In His Word we find answers today;
Open the Bible, surely will lead the way.
Hearing what Jesus wants us to do,
Turn to Micah 6:8 in a nutshell for me and you.

[written in 1985]

Precious Gift

The Word of God is so precious,
Sweet as days of old; delicious.
Most precious gift we can hold,
In Genesis, beautiful creation behold.

Adam had dominion over all,
Didn't obey, causing us to fall.
Adam gave the animals a nice name.
Fellowship with God,
On and on, up and downs;
God called prophets to see.

Much, much later God sent His only Son to Earth,
Fulfilling prophecy by virgin birth.
When He grew and grew, became a Man,
Walked, talked, lived, and loved and—

In due time, obeyed God, a living sacrifice;
Paid wages of sin—what a price!
We sinners knew not,
far from God and full of sin,
God's Son's blood cleansed, restored,
Brings back us to Him.

[written in 1967]

He Is God

He is God—now I ask, isn't
That the most precious gift anyone can receive?
A sinner lost and far from Him can believe?
All one has to do believe, confess, accept forgiveness?
Gone; forgives, forgets life's whole mess.

His Holy Spirit leads, guides, so much more;
Tells us to tell and in Revelation 3:20,
Show scriptures, He is the Door.
John 10 is a good chapter. Concordance,
Study, pray, helps us more.
"Amen! Amen!"

B-I-B-L-E
[1965]

Bible
Inspires
Blood
Loves
Everyone

B-I-B-L-E
[1967]

Bible for all walks of life;
Inspired is every word.
Blessings fall on poor and sick alike.
Love is our God, the one and true God;
Everyone can receive God's salvation.

B-I-B-L-E
[1978]

Bible most bloody Book
Is important, just look.
Blood cleanses even today;
Love letter when read leads the way;
Eternity given one sweet day.

B-I-B-L-E
[1982]

Bible written ages apart,
In our soul, mind, and heart,
Bible verses stored cometh when needed—1 Corinthians 10:13.
Love is a word that plants a seed,
Even written centuries ago.

B-I-B-L-E
[1989]

Bible written, author is God Almighty,
Inspired men of His to write.
Blood in O.T. and N.T. need no longer shed,
Love is first all the way to Revelation,
Every book written as one voice.

Bible harmonizes all the way through,
Inspires me as well as you.
Blood harmonized from Old to New
Love of God weaves from Genesis to Revelation
Everyone is in need of
Christ's salvation.

B-I-B-L-E
[2020]

Bible is a Goldmine,
In time God worked fine;
But I did not know,
Let His Word just flow,
Even to a Book "Go!"

B-I-B-L-E
[2021]

Bible is a Goldmine;
Instead sharing now, not before
Blood of Christ opened door.
Love comes ever so fine,
Even as He and I write.

B-I-B-L-E
[April, 2021]

Bible, fresh as today's news,
Inspires me and you.
Love of God flows to one another,
Blood of Christ makes us a sister or brother.
Every one He sweetly calls, "Come."

As we all work to help build up God's kingdom:
"Come, ye who heavy laden"—Matthew 11:28.
"Come, ye without money"—Isaiah 55:1–3.
None left out—2 Peter 3:9.
Taste the Lord—Psalm 34:8.
Pray: two or three, I'm in the midst, saith the Lord.

Idols

Today's idols not as days of old,
But we like more than God
Whatever we put before Savior, our Lord.

But with Christ He forgives 24/7;
Sent His Holy Spirit to lead to heaven,
And help us day by day.
Amazing, closes and opens another door as I pray,
Nor had I given thought about a pen
Nor how the Bible began.
Idols led the Jews away.
Now really, why we do pray?
This I took for granted,
Just part of Bible—
Idols came as no-no.

[written in 2021]

Beauty

Beauty from ashes in Isaiah 61;
Each desire, Psalm 37:4.
Beauty is another word for cleaning,
After we confess sin to Christ.

1 John 1:9 is a beautiful verse,
And also 2 Corinthians 5:17;
Romans chapter 12, beauty as thirst.

Not beauty as beauty world has and fade,
Beauty everlasting, God's Son He gave.
An inward beauty shines, an outward glow
As Holy Spirit teaches us to obey: "Go."

B-E-A-U-T-Y
Beauty to believers,
Everyone who is a receiver.
All it takes knowing Christ,
Us cry out so very sorry (sin)
To God Almighty.
Yes, believing in God's Son,
"Now, that's real beauty!"

[written in 1977]

Abundant Life

Abundant life is given by God alone—Acts 4:12,
Made all possible when He left His throne.
To come to this sad, worthless, sin Earth
In the form of His virgin birth.
Abundant life given to all who believe,
Not just a few who repent and receive.
The invitation, "Come 24/7." Unbelievers, is that you?

He came to redeem red, black, yellow, brown, and white;
Take darkness of sin, lost in Son who is light.
Plant us on a solid foundation
As soon as we accept His salvation.

None left out—Matthew 11:28;
Come small, medium, mute, big, fat, tall, and short.
Come to His salvation;
There will be rejoicing,
There will be singing
In heaven as angels sing the joyful song,
"A sinner has come home."

[written in 1982]

There Is No Other

Jesus Christ, there is no other—Acts 4:12;
Why not come too, as a sister or a brother?
In the family of the Almighty God
Who gave His only Son as Savior and Lord—John 3:16, Romans 5:8.
Haven't we tried a lot? Of this and that?
Found the world is not where it is at;
The yearning within hasn't been filled, so hard to explain.

Surprise! As a sinner can be filled by God's plan;
Find no longer emptiness within the soul.
God's Son at the cross filled the hungry hole,
In God's eyes we are as white as snow.
Justify? What is that? Just as if never sin;
His precious blood took our sin.
Far as east is from west,
As soon as we believe, repent, and confess,
He does all the rest.

[written in 1967]

The Messiah

The Old Testament tells how the Jews long
For their Messiah to come along.
New Testament tells a star shone so bright
Shepherds saw God-appointed night.

Angels harmonizing, singing "Peace on Earth,"
Announcing God has sent His Son by virgin birth.
Christ, the Messiah born above all men,
Not in a home nor a hospital but outside an inn.

They knew not history that night proclaimed,
Fulfilling all prophets had claimed.
A virgin shall be Messiah's mother,
God's holy line—Judah, David, Abraham—Acts 4:12—read no other.

[written in 1972]

Sabbath Worship Home

God created the beautiful earth—Genesis 1:1,
I can enjoy and rejoice in God's virgin birth.
His Son sent so sinners can be free—Matthew 1:18;
Unique amongst animals, meal, and hay,
Homemade crib, asleep as Babe lay.

God gave His commandments as a school teacher,
We see His only Son fulfilled them to a T.
Also, God created, He worked six days;
He rested the seventh from all He had done.
Blessed Sabbath; let's read it in Genesis,
Then later, His Son fulfilled as Christ.
Obedience became a living sacrifice;
Gave His life for atonement of sin.
Many blessings we rejoice and enjoy because of Him.

[written in 1999]

COVID-19

Because of COVID-19 can't go to church anymore;
I know God will open a door—
If all Christians will stay true to Him,
Ask forgiveness—to forgive us of our sin.
Now COVID-19 is here; not safe to go anywhere.
Time to get things done,
Thank GOD we know His Son.

Lord, What Can I Do?

In prayer, Lord, what can I do?
Oh! Lord, what should I do?
"Write my Word as ye study day or night;
I am with all in darkness shedding light.
Call many confusions all around,
Ye know love and grace abound," saith the Lord.

"Take daily a walk or two,
That's something ye can do.
Just sit outdoors too,
Continue to read My Word day by day.

Call two or three; yes, know, I am in the midst when you pray
—Matthew 18:20;
Take a nap; ye will feel better.
Get ready to send many a letter.
"Sit, relax, spend time with me," saith the Lord.

[written in 1999]

The Bible Now

Well, we have to eat each day,
The Bible feeds as we pray.
In a mirror have to look or I'm a mess,
If not read God's Word, Satan steps in nevertheless.

God never promised life would be sailing,
But would be with us, never leaving—Hebrews 13:5.
A way would be made—John 14:6, 1 Corinthians 10:13.

Oh! Lord, I'm so weak, You are so strong,
Help me I pray—1 Corinthians 4:10, Matthew 6:6.
I find what I am going through
Not as bad as I thought.
In His time found V-I-C-T-O-R-Y,
All because He gave all at C-A-L-V-A-R-Y.

And God continues to give more;
May close but opens another door.
Bible written way back when,
His Word lives on, never end.

[written in 2021]

Today Now

Today—right up to today,
Yes, the Word of God answers mankind!
God wipes believer's slate clean, we find
There's no sin His blood doesn't cover.
No matter how bad, "Come!" He repeats over and over.

There's not one thing we need to suffer alone—1 Corinthians 10:13.
Christ's precious blood does atone.
The invitation "24/7 Come as you are"—Matthew 11:28,
Night, early morn of day,
All one has to do is pray.
Study, if not, read His Word; Holy Spirit living within
Each day find drawing nearer to Him.
He will supply all spiritual need;
Telling another may plant His seed.

To grow takes a need of dedication.
Ask Him what, how to surrender?
Find a believing church
Puts Christ head, center as thirst.

Now That You Are Saved

We are:

2 Corinthians 5:17

Therefore, if anyone is in Christ, he is a new creation;
old things have passed away; behold, all things have become new.

John 1:12

But as many as received Him,
to them He gave the right to become children of God,
to those who believe in His name.

John 1:13

Who were born, not of blood, nor the will of the flesh,
nor of the will of man, but of God.

Ephesians 2:8

For by grace you have been saved through faith,
and that not of yourselves; it is the gift of God.

Ephesians 2:9

Not of works,
lest anyone should boast.

Ephesians 2:10

For we are his workmanship,
created in Christ Jesus
unto good works,
which God hath before ordained that we should walk in them.

Ephesians 2:19

Now therefore
ye are no more strangers and foreigners,
but fellow citizens with the saints, and of the household of God.

Ephesians 1:7

In whom
we have redemption through his blood,
the forgiveness of sins, according to the riches of his grace.

Ephesians 3:17

That Christ
may dwell
in your hearts
by faith; that ye, being rooted and grounded in love.

Ephesians 4:25

Wherefore putting away lying,
speak every man truth
with his neighbor:
for we are members one of another.

Galatians 5:1

Stand fast
therefore in the liberty
wherewith Christ
hath made us free, and be not
entangled again
with the yoke of bondage.

Please read prayerfully
Galatians 5:16–26
Very important to you: Romans, John, and Isaiah
Amen!

[written in 1992]

Devotions Outline, Galatians 3:1–25

Open to Galatians 3 verse 25,
Yes, my friend, Christ is alive.
World is saying, "God is dead."
Yes, world is waxing worse.

Verse 1: O foolish unbeliever,
Not seen,
Not heard.

Verse 2: Choice
a. Believe = faith
b. Not = works

Verse 3: So foolish
a. By flesh
b. Only way

Verse 4: Believing
In vain

Verse 5: He who ministers
a. In spirit
b. Miracles
c. Doeth
d. By Law
e. Faith
(Reminds in the book of James)

Verse 6: Abraham
a. Believed

Verse 7: We too
a. Children of Abraham

Amen! Amen!

Verse 8: God's promise
a. Justify
b. Shall
c. All nations
d. Be blessed

Verses 9–10: Under law
a. Works
b. Cursed
c. Not justified

Verse 13: Christ
a. Redeemed
b. Us
c. From the curse of the law

Verse 11: Just shall live by Faith

Verse 14: Abraham's blessings
a. Come to Gentiles
b. Believe the promise
c. Spirit by faith

Verses 15–16: No man can change it
a. Confirmed
b. Abraham's seed too numerous to count

Verses 17–19: God gave
a. Ordained
b. Witness
c. By angels

Verse 20: Mediator
   a. God
   b. By prayer

Verses 21–23: Who believe the law
   a. Shut up

Verses 24–25: No longer
   a. Wrapped up
   b. In Christ

Verse 26: Poem
Almost hear music in background.

We no longer live under law,
We live B-E-C-A-U-S-E of Christ
Who never wanders away.
Hallelujah! Hallelujah!
(Chorus)
Christ opened the way for us,
Obeyed, not one flaw, not one sin;
The Son of God did it all for Him.

His name so meaningful,
No deeds can be matched;
All He is, was, ever will be.
To every nation Savior, Lord,
We sing joyfully praises to Thee.

Change My Mind

I almost didn't come to the Goldmine;
Last-minute decision I changed my mind.
Just didn't feel like digging today
'Cause I was down a bit.
But may find a nugget on my way.
I did! I did!

An axe cuts in two O.T. and N.T.
Bible may speak to me today.
Calvary heard; sins gone when pray.
Deliverance washes white as snow.
Everyone, Christ came to redeem us.
Faith received by His loving touch,
God is the one and true living God.
How and why do I have to go?—"Go where?"
Intercedes God's Son for us 24/7;
Jesus leads believers to heaven.
Key opens all spirit matter,
Love starts, never ends.

Message and theme speaks in one voice,
None to be left out—look!—Matthew 11:28.
Obey and trust go hand in hand.
Passover and Pentecost same day? No! No!
Quiet time renews strength;
Righteousness in exchange for rags,
Savior to some becomes "Lord of Life!"
Trust and truth go hand in hand;
"Under His Wings," more than song.
V-I-C-T-O-R-Y to overcome,
Washes white as snow.
X equals Greek for Jesus.
You and I weaved throughout the Bible;
Zeal and zealous—which will it be?

So glad I changed my mind;
In the Bible I did find.
Know not what God has for me,
Truly now I know I can praise Thee.

[written in March, 2021]

Filled to the Brim

The Bible is filled to the brim,
More branches clinging to a limb;
The Bible holds and's filled with truth,
No rots, decay, nor spotted fruit.

More is locked up and sealed,
Hard to see, not easy to be revealed;
Tells all we possibly can't comprehend,
Begins before began and will never end.

The Bible explains so clear we should understand
We need His wisdom, knowledge, and
His Holy Spirit opens heart, mind, and soul,
Begins to fill up spiritual bowl.

The Bible not only everyone's favorite book
But comes alive—speaks as look.
Reveals ever so much more,
Revelation 3:20 says, "Knock at the door."

From Genesis to Revelation is one theme,
Tells the whole story all about Him.
And so full of love and forgiveness,
24/7 waiting to rid us of life's mess.

From the overflowing filled bowl,
In itself a message to be told;
For us to drink and chew,
So, meaningful to our soul, too.

Read, study, walk, talk, do, and pray keeps us whole.
Scripture John 14:6—He is the Truth, Life, and Way.
As we have daily devotions and pray,
We see love and forgiveness as we forgive one another.

His Holy Spirit will keep us awake;
The cry be, "It is never too late."
Find Bible, is not so hard to read,
May find Jesus helps us to plant His seed.

Fill us from His bowl to brim,
Both bowls filled to overflowing.
So many blessings keep us going,
With a message, "Come" helps us to build His kingdom.
Amen! Amen!

Scriptures tell verses:
1) 2 Timothy 3:16
All of John 15

2) Daniel 12:9
Ephesians 4:30
Revelation 5:1–10
Proverbs 8:22–31
(Proverbs 8:32–36 establish in beginning)

3) Proverbs 4:5
James 5:16

4) Please read John 10
Revelation 3:20

5) Genesis 3:15
Romans 5:8
John 3:16
Matthew 26:28
Luke 24:47

6) 1 Thessalonians 5:19

7) Luke 17:4
1 Corinthians 13

8) 2 Corinthians 5:17
Ephesians 2:18–22

9) Romans 13:11
1 Corinthians 15:3–4
Matthew 11:28
John 15:3, 12–17

10) Matthew 5:3
Romans 14:17
John 3:3
John 18:36
Daniel 4:3
Other verses (I just didn't study all with concordance).

[written January 4, 2021]

Thanksgiving

Thanksgiving is all one can eat,
Giving thanks for such a lovely feast.
But isn't that what worldly do?
Step out in faith, do what Jesus would do:

He was always thinking about others;
Never faulted nor yielded to any sin.
Let's make this Thanksgiving a rememberable day;
Do more than give thanks as we journey His way.

Kind of think we lost true meaning,
Or am I waking up and learning?
"It is better to give than receive,"
Means more to me then when I first did believe.

[written in 2020]

Love Story is Love Letter

Bible is a love story,
Went down as history.
The Written Word lives on and on,
Fresh as newspaper read early morn.

God's love, faith, mercy, and grace constantly abound,
Though all races had ups and downs.
The Bible tells all the good and bad;
God gave to His creatures all He had.

Prophets He chose, spoke as voice one,
Love began in Genesis 1:1.
Notice as read: God created all men would need
To fulfill hunger and thirst,
Beauty was found blooming forth from earth.

Man: male and female not on Earth,
God made Adam in His image first.
And the Jews' life began,
GOD raised Moses to do,
Promises of God came ever so true.

All this time did not know all were sinners; far from God.
In due time, God's appointed time,
He sent His Son, Saviour as Lord.
Read or heard about God's love,
Shown visible flew and landed a dove.

The Word of God took on a new meaning,
Through God's Son found a learning
Who, and what His Father is, and was—Love.
Jesus healed, helped, and did so much.

At Calvary suffered untold for us,
Each of God's creatures full of sin,
Need to repent, confess, and believe Him;
He sent His Holy Spirit to live within.

The New Testament filled with Love—1 Corinthians 13 tells all.
Read Psalms, Genesis 3:15 and Isaiah 53.
Open your heart and read, study, or look,
Verses after verses filled with love.
Instruction given in love;
Armor can wear every day;
24/7 open is the door;
God will meet needs;
Never leave us.
These are just a beginning
To show forth God's love.
Yes, Bible is a love letter,
God's love to us.
NEVER: A beginning.
NEVER: An ending.

[written April 1, 2021]

Into Goldmine Go!

Into Goldmine go,
Others from states flow.
All in need, money doesn't last;
Just like came year past.

Have to dig, dig, and dig each day,
Not like a job, get weekly pay.
For mankind God created Goldmine
To enjoy beauty and precious gems I find.

Seems more go home with empty hand,
Some so discouraged, angry, and
Give up dream of owning land;
Not everyone gets rich as some do.

In the Goldmine, hear sweet note,
A poem put to music someone wrote.
"I may not find any gold,"
I found more a clean soul.
In the Bible Goldmine,
Love and grace I find.

Peace, joy, my sins gone;
Christ forgave, forgot as I walk alone.
I found Christ worth more than gold,
I found He washes whiter than snow.

[written in 2021]

Psalm 51 for Today

Truly find David loved God.
He cried out to the one living Lord
"Blot out my transgression,"
Knowing God knew the whole situation.

And God could forgive and forget,
Though he, himself, would remember and regret.
Psalm 51 can be applied to our heart, soul, and mind,
Jesus, God's Son, is the Savior Divine.

Came to wash us white as snow,
Make us aware in Him we can grow.
Like David, we have to believe,
Confess sin so we, too, can receive.

[written February 28, 1972]

91st Psalm Shadow

Shadow, what does it do?
Follow around me and you.
Always found and abide,
Can be fat, narrow, small, thin, or wide.

Shadow is with us day by day,
Doesn't care how we walk, good or bad.
Nevertheless, it leads the way.
Things get worse or we are glad.

Mama knew a poem,
"Sitting on Ma's Knee."
Can't remember it for the life of me.
Shadow cost nothing, always free,
Shadow does follow you as well as me.

If my brother were here, I would ask him,
Always was humming or singing.
(Know it had a catchy tune.)

My Friend, Don

My friend Don said, "One day at a time."
I discouraged and sad, "God will work it out fine."—Romans 8:28.
You believe, are one of His branches—John 15.

God knows every problem, cry, and heartache—1 Corinthians 10:13.
Is teaching us something about
GOD'S
RIGHTEOUSNESS
AT
CHRIST'S
EXPENSE
(I'm not forgotten—4/10/2021)

Truly need to take one day at time,
He takes every sin of mine.
My favorite is John 1:12,
And next in line is 1 John 1:9–10.

Not Don's poem, took what he said,
As he witnessed of Christ.
God and I wrote a poem.
1963 gave me—while teaching
His adult class.
I think I will share
As I claim Psalm 37:4.

Not in high school book 1954
No short story nor a joke,
No poem either,
I wanted leave for underclass.

Like so many do—
Here goes what I wrote while teaching on "HOME"
(Very first Poem 1963.)
"HOME!"
The home not just a house on a street;
The home is where living a treat.
It brings happiness and joy to all;
If Christ not the head, it will fall.

God speak of home, a family life,
Rules for children, husband and wife.
It's not only shelter, security and life exist;
It's to be a school where children are taught.

To love God, honesty, truthful manners are caught,
Where devotions, singing and praying each day,
And little ones learning to pray.
Do we live our faith and thirst?
Or leave our belief in church?
Would be not for one to guess
If God is head of a home,
Always the unseen guest.

***

Taught Adult Class
Year 1963
At Seventh-day Adventist Church
Bridgton, Maine
This is first poem
God gave me.
Now, 2021 writing
To please Thee.
Gives me two lines,
His hand on mine.

[written in 1965]

Message to Tell

Ministers, pastors, missionaries, and believers,
Prophets, kings, leaders, and followers.
Yes, all and disciples spoke as
One voice—"Repent."
Even today, people heed not one word, own way went.

Way back when, Eve listened to a false leader—Genesis 3:13.
Did she not? What happened?
She gave fruit to Adam—Genesis 3:6.
They both knew but forgot God spoke.

What happened? Disobey God—Genesis 3:9–10.
Result of disobedience? Genesis 3:23–24.
Later whole world wicked—Genesis 6:5.
Result wickedness—Genesis 6:7.
Was that the end of men on Earth—
Yes or no?
Answer in verse 8.
God had a heart of God—verse 13.
Accomplish overcome hate—Verse 14.
Did men repent, yes or no?
Verse 16—God full control.
Verse 17—Result—Verse 22.
God's promise 8:21.

[written in 1968]

Message, Part 2

Some years past Pharaoh feared—Exodus 1:22.
God saw He has a sense of humor briefly.
It was Pharaoh's daughter that saved Moses;
Her father tried to kill boy babies,
The very ones—Moses was one of them.
Moses's own sister saved, own mother got paid to nurse—Exodus 2:8.
Pharaoh, himself, taught war to Moses.

Pharaoh raised—GOD called, used Moses,
Used him as God's people leader.
God had Moses free captivity of Israel out of Pharaoh's control.

The one theme story, Moses leads,
Joshua follows.
Judah—Judges 1; called Simeon—Judges 1:3.
Then judges follow, cried a king—Saul, David.

Too deep for me the prophets, more interested that Messiah came.

[written April 10, 2021]

Haven't Thought

Part 1
Haven't thought much about
Bible filled with faith not doubt.
They had no Bible like us today,
It was written a little each day.

And it happens good and bad,
Every emotion as God spoke that day.
Prophets heeded call to do God's will,
Chosen to live rough times and people tell.

[written August 1, 1983]

Part 2
In the light I hadn't thought,
More precious is my Bible.
God, Creation,
S-A-L-V-A-T-I-O-N,
God's Son,
Savior,
Acknowledge
Love
Victory
At
Tomb
In
Obedience
None should perish.

[written April 14, 2021]

G-R-A-C-E

Hallelujah! Finally did what someone did with G-R-A-C-E.
God's
Righteousness
At
Christ's
Expense

[written April 14, 2021]

Bible Written [1979]

Bible written for all walks of life;
Believers underline verse or verses as Holy Spirit sheds light.
As Christians read, study, and write therein,
Unbelievers believe not about nor fear Him.

Bible Written [1983]

Bible written so long ago
Is as fresh as morning news hold.
Sweet as a honeycomb,
Appointed time will take us home.

Bible written travels everywhere,
Can be read 24/7, sitting in a chair.
Weaved through it God's awesome love.
When we thirst, He quenches our thirst.

Food for our hungry soul,
Comfort when lonely and sad;
With us in illness, sickness, even in sorrow,
We know Him who holds tomorrow.

Bible Written
[1989]

Bible written author is God Almighty,
Inspiring men of old to write;
Blood greatest sacrifice in Old and New Testament.
Love started in Genesis all the way to Revelation,
Every book written ages apart speaks in one voice.

Bible written harmonizes, such pretty music;
Inspires and uplifts Old as New.
Blessings flow out even today to me and you,
Love letter if follow leads the way.
Everyone can be washed at Calvary,
Yes, even called today—Matthew 11:28;
An invitation today—2 Corinthians 6:2.

As We Study a Bit

As we study a little bit,
Old Testament and New Testament closely fit.
Yes, harmonize a smooth song
Within all humans can belong.

Let's turn to Genesis 3:15: first Jesus is mentioned.
Surprise: read Proverbs 8:22 to verse 31.
Don't stop there; in same chapter speaking is God's Son,
Start at verse 6 and end verse 21.

Weren't you surprised to see what we just saw?
God planned before Genesis 1 verse 1 beginning.

Now turn to N.T. in Gospel of John 1:1;
Centuries past years came, years ago, harmonize in unity.

If I could write music notes, a song would be
"Old Testament and New Testament, Claiming Jesus, the Messiah, is He."
Just repent! Just believe!
All humans can relieve.

No doubt Romans 5:8,
In our day John 3:16 relate.
Harmonize Old Testament and New Testament in unity and love,
As our hand fits into a glove.

Postscript

You will see from time to time a little, I don't have good grammar, but it is just little ol' me. Big I as it should be, standing for God, the Three in One.

We invite you to view the complete
selection of titles we publish at:
www.TEACHServices.com

We encourage you to write us
with your thoughts about this,
or any other book we publish at:
info@TEACHServices.com

TEACH Services' titles may be purchased in
bulk quantities for educational, fund-raising,
business, or promotional use.
bulksales@TEACHServices.com

Finally, if you are interested in seeing
your own book in print, please contact us at:
publishing@TEACHServices.com
We are happy to review your manuscript at no charge.

www.ingramcontent.com/pod-product-compliance
Lightning Source LLC
Chambersburg PA
CBHW070558160426
43199CB00014B/2543